Knitted
Animal Socks

Knitted
Animal Socks

6 novelty patterns for cute creature socks

Lauren Riker

sewandso

www.sewandso.co.uk

CONTENTS

INTRODUCTION

Give your feet the ultimate treat with this collection of adorable knitted animal socks!

These colourful socks are guaranteed to brighten your day with their cute faces and adorable ears. Not only are these socks full of character from the front, but each animal design also features a fun message on the heel, making them extra special. When knitting your new pair of furry friends, you can also work a contrast toe, heel, or both, for added style.

Whether you choose to knit a pair of cat, owl, panda, koala, fox, or pig socks in ankle or knee-high length, you are sure to find an option that suits you and all of your loved ones.

You can have loads of fun playing around with alternative colourways and if you're feeling adventurous you could even design your own unique animal sock.

Enjoy!

HOW TO USE THIS BOOK

Follow the steps below before you start knitting your socks.

Step 1 Read the Tools and Materials section, which specifies the type of yarn to use and the recommended needle sizes.

Step 2 Check your tension (gauge) following the instructions provided (see Tension) to make sure you are knitting to the required tension, otherwise your socks will not fit.

Step 3 Check the size chart (see Size Chart) and choose the correct size to knit.

Step 4 Read through the Techniques section to familiarise yourself with the basic stitches and techniques used (see Techniques).

Step 5 Choose your project, and when finished, don't forget to block your socks (see Techniques : Blocking).

TOOLS AND MATERIALS

YARN

4ply sock yarn is recommended as the best yarn to use. Sock yarn can also be classed as 'fingering' weight and is generally a mix of wool and nylon, for flexibility and durability. You can choose sock yarn that is machine washable (labelled as superwash wool) or you can choose sock yarn that requires handwashing.

The yarn used for all of the socks in this book is Knit Picks Stroll Sock Yarn which is 75% superwash merino wool with 25% nylon. Each ball weighs 50g and is 211m/231yds in length. Quantities required for each pair of socks are specified within each pattern.

NEEDLES

For sock knitting, a set of 4 double-pointed needles (dpns) are recommended, in size 2.75mm (US 2) for the main sock (or size needed to achieve the correct tension), plus a set of size 2.25mm (US 1) dpns for the cuff and a single 3.75mm (US 5) needle for casting off loosely.

OTHER USEFUL EQUIPMENT

A pair of sharp scissors – for snipping yarn.

A hard, see-through ruler – for measuring tension.

A tape measure – for measuring the length of longer pieces of knitting.

A wool/tapestry needle – blunt ended (a pointy needle will split your yarn and spoil your knitting).

Sock blockers – for blocking your socks.

Stitch markers – to mark the start of the round (optional).

Stitch holder – to hold stitches when not being worked on the needles.

Row counter – helpful to keep a note of how many rows you've knitted.

Notebook and pen – as an alternative to a row counter, or to make notes of your tension or any alterations or adaptations you make to a pattern.

Project bag – perfect for keeping your work and equipment in.

TENSION

Before starting your socks you will need to knit up a tension (gauge) swatch. This is necessary so that your socks will fit snuggly and not end up either too big or too small.

Your knitted swatch will need to mirror the circular knitting of the socks and cannot be knitted flat as your tension will not be the same when knitting flat, compared to when knitting in the round. This is because when you work stocking stitch in the round, only knit stitches are used, whereas when you work stocking stitch flat, both knit and purl stitches are used. Tension can be different when knitting these two stitches, so they can be slightly different in size and they can also use different amounts of yarn.

HOW TO MEASURE TENSION

Cast on the number of stitches that you need for your chosen sock size. Knit in the round for approximately 10cm (4in). Cast off. Lay your knitted tube on a flat surface. Place a see-through ruler vertically across the tube and measure how many stitches and rows there are to 2.5cm (1in).

For all socks in this book, tension should be:

7.75 sts and 10.5 rows to measure 2.5 x 2.5cm (1 x 1in) using 2.75mm needles over stocking stitch (worked in the round).

This equates to:

31 sts and 42 rows to measure 10 x 10cm (4 x 4in) using 2.75mm needles over stocking stitch (worked in the round).

If your stitch and row counts are the same as specified above, you can go ahead and start knitting. If you have more stitches and rows, you are knitting too tightly and your socks will end up too small. You'll need to make another swatch with slightly larger needles (and measure again).

If you have fewer stitches than specified, you are knitting too loosely and your socks will be too big. You'll need to make another swatch with slightly smaller needles and measure again.

Continue to swatch with different sized needles until you achieve the correct tension stated, and make sure that you always use this needle size for the main part of your socks.

Use the chart opposite to determine the most appropriate size to knit.

SIZE CHART

Ankle socks can be made in sizes **XS:S:M:L:XL.**
Long socks can be made in sizes **S:M:L:XL.**
Smallest size is written first with larger sizes in brackets, e.g. XS(S:M:L:XL).
Sock height is specified in each pattern.

Size	XS	S	M	L	XL
Age (estimate)	3-5 years	5-9 years	7-12 years	Adult S/M	Adult M/L
Foot length	15-17.5cm (6-7in)	17.5-20cm (7-8in)	21-23cm (8¼-9¼in)	22-24cm (8¾-9¾in)	25-27cm (9¾-10¾in)
Finished foot circumference	14.5cm (5¾in)	16cm (6¼in)	17cm (6¾in)	18.5cm (7¼in)	19.5cm (7¾in)

ABBREVIATIONS
(see Techniques for detailed stitch instructions)

dpn(s)	double-pointed needle(s)
k	knit
kfb	knit into the front and back of the next st (to increase 1 st)
k2tog	knit 2 sts together (to decrease 1 st)
p	purl
psso	pass slipped stitch over knitted stitch (to decrease 1 st)
rnd(s)	round(s)
sl	slip
ssk	slip next 2 sts, one at a time, to the right-hand needle then knit them both together through the back loops (to decrease 1 st)
st(s)	stitch(es)
W&T	wrap and turn

Foxy Lady
ANKLE SOCKS

The fun starts here with these foxy socks! Full of personality, these cute creatures will delight anyone you knit them for. You can adapt the lettering to suit a child or a man, so you can make matching pairs for the whole family. Alternatively, why not substitute the orange shade for grey or even pale blue for a winter look?

SIZES

XS(S:M:L:XL) – see Size Chart for detailed measurements.
Sock Height: 14.5(15.75:17:17:18.5)cm (5¾(6¼:6¾:6¾:7¼)in).

DIFFICULTY LEVEL

TENSION

31 sts and 42 rows to measure 10 x 10cm (4 x 4in), over stocking stitch, using 2.75mm (US 2) needles (or size needed to achieve correct tension).

You will need

Yarn

Knit Picks Stroll Sock Yarn, 50g (211m/231yds), 75% superwash merino wool, 25% nylon, in the following shades:

- 1 ball of Pumpkin, shade 23699 (MC)
- 36.5m/40yds of White, shade 26082 (CC1)
- 5.5m/6yds of Black, shade 23701 (CC2)

Needles

- 2.25mm (US 1) double-pointed needles (set of 4) or circular needle
- 2.75mm (US 2) double-pointed needles (set of 4) or circular needle
- 3.75mm (US 5) needle (only used for loose cast off)

Extras

- Stitch holder
- Stitch marker
- Wool/tapestry needle

Pattern Notes

For all techniques used in this pattern, refer to Techniques for full instructions.

Socks are worked from the toe up.

Instructions are given for using double-pointed needles. If using a circular needle for the magic loop method, note that the instructions have the heel split over Needles 1 and 2, and the instep on Needle 3.

FOXY SOCKS (MAKE TWO ALIKE)

TOE

Use Judy's Magic Cast-on method (see Techniques).

With 2.75mm needles and Pumpkin (MC), cast on 16(20:20:24:24)sts over 2 needles – 8(10:10:12:12)sts on each needle.

Rnd 1 Knit.

Next, divide the 8(10:10:12:12)sts on first needle evenly over 2 dpns for the bottom of sock/heel. These are now called Needle 1 and Needle 2. Leave the last 8(10:10:12:12)sts on third dpn for top of sock/instep. This is now called Needle 3.

Now start increase rounds as follows (see Techniques: Toe Increases).

Rnd 2 Starting with Needle 1: kfb, knit to last st on Needle 2, kfb in last st; on Needle 3: kfb, knit to last st on Needle 3, kfb in last st – 20(24:24:28:28)sts.

Rep **Rnds 1-2** until you have 44(48:52:56:60)sts in total.

FOOT

For a generic foot size, knit until foot measures approximately 12.75(15.25:17.75:19:21)cm (5(6:7:7½:8¼)in) from cast on, or for best fit, knit until foot measures 3.75(3.75:4.5:4.5:4.5)cm (1½(1½:1¾:1¾:1¾)in) less than your total foot length.

HEEL

Change to White (CC1) and work in rows over Needles 1 & 2. See Techniques: Wrap and Turn for W&T.

Bottom half of heel

Row 1 Starting with Needle 1: knit to last st on Needle 2, W&T.

Row 2 Purl to last st on Needle 1 (this is last st with wrong side facing), W&T.

Row 3 Knit to 1 st before the last wrapped st of the heel, W&T.

Row 4 Purl to 1 st before the last wrapped st of the heel, W&T.

Rep **Rows 3-4** until 6(8:8:8:10)sts remain unworked in the middle of the heel. Bottom half of heel is now complete.

Top half of heel

See Techniques: Wrap and Turn for picking up wrapped stitches.

Row 1 Knit to first wrapped st, pick up wrapped st and knit it together with st on needle, W&T the next st (this st now has 2 wraps).

Row 2 Purl to first wrapped st, pick up wrapped st and purl it together with st on needle, W&T the next st (this st now has 2 wraps).

Row 3 Knit to st with double wrap. Pick up both wraps and knit them together with st on needle, W&T the next st.

Row 4 Purl to st with double wrap. Pick up both wraps and purl them together with st on needle, W&T the next st.

Rep **Rows 3-4** until there is 1 double wrap left on each side of heel.

Change to Pumpkin (MC) (note that the first stitch will be skipped when working this row).

Next row Rep **Row 3**, wrapping 1 st from top of sock/instep.

Next row Rep **Row 4**, wrapping 1 st from top of sock/ instep.

LEG

Rnd 1 Begin to knit sock in the round again. When you come to the wrapped sts on the instep, pick up these wraps and knit them together with their respective sts.

Continue until sock measures 12.75(14:15.25:15.25:16.5)cm (5(5½:6:6:6½)in) from bottom of heel, or desired length, noting that ribbing will add 2cm (¾in).

Fox Face for sizes M–XL

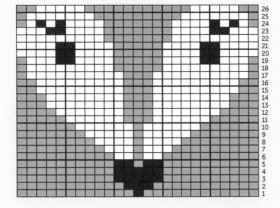

MC ▨   CC1 ▢   CC2 ■

Fox Face for sizes XS–S

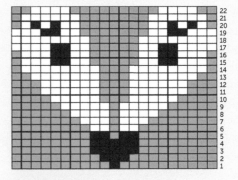

Fox Heel for all sizes

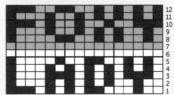

CUFF

Change to 2.25mm needles and work in (k1, p1) rib for 2cm (¾in), working to last 1(2:2:2:2)sts on last round.

EARS

When casting off in rib (see Techniques: Casting Off in Rib), you will need to cast off very loosely to ensure your sock will fit your leg, so a much larger needle is recommended – try using a 3.75mm needle to cast off for the perfect tension.

If you want to cast off loosely using your own preferred method, feel free to ignore the needle changing instructions referenced. If knitting for yourself you can try the sock on before knitting the ears to make sure you are happy with your casting off tension.

With 3.75mm needle, cast off the next 1(2:2:2:2)sts, then cast off all sts on Needles 1 & 2, and cast off 1(2:2:2:2)sts from Needle 3 – 20(20:22:24:26)sts remaining (including 1 st on right-hand needle).

Change back to 2.25mm needles and work in rib as established for 8 sts (9 sts are now on right-hand needle). Place these 9 sts just worked onto a stitch holder.

With 3.75mm needle, cast off 2(2:4:6:8)sts, change to 2.25mm needles and work in rib as established for the last 8 sts – 9 sts remaining.

Left ear

Using a second 2.25mm needle, pick up 9 sts behind 9 sts just worked (see Techniques: Ears, picking up stitches for ears) – 18 sts.

Change to 2.75mm needles. Work in the round, starting at one side of ear, using a stitch marker to mark the start of the round.

Work left ear following instructions given for pointed ears (see Techniques: Ears).

Right ear

Transfer 9 sts from stitch holder to a 2.25mm needle. Using a second 2.25mm needle, pick up 9 sts behind the 9 live sts (see Techniques: Ears, picking up stitches for ears) – 18 sts.

Change to 2.75mm needles. Work in the round, starting at one side of ear.

Work right ear following instructions given for pointed ears (see Techniques: Ears).

ADDING DETAILS

Using duplicate stitch (see Techniques: Duplicate Stitch), embroider colour charts onto socks as follows:

Face

Choose face chart according to size knitted and apply on centre front of sock, to sit 2 rows below ribbing.

Heel

Apply heel chart on centre back heel, using contrast heel as a guide.

FINISHING

Weave all ends into wrong side and trim.

Block the socks (see Techniques: Blocking).

If knitting socks for a child or man, you can choose not to add the lettering. Alternatively, just apply the word 'foxy' and omit the word 'lady'.

~Oink Oink~
ANKLE SOCKS

Keep your little piggies warm and happy in these cheeky socks that are full of character. These lovable farmyard friends will keep your feet as warm as toast when you head off to market for your groceries. You could switch from pink to grey, or use beige for a more natural tone.

SIZES

XS(S:M:L:XL) – see Size Chart for detailed measurements.
Sock Height: 14.5(15.75:17:17:18.5)cm (5¾(6¼:6¾:6¾:7¼)in).

DIFFICULTY LEVEL

TENSION

31 sts and 42 rows to measure 10 x 10cm (4 x 4in), over stocking stitch, using 2.75mm needles (or size needed to achieve correct tension).

You will need

Yarn

Knit Picks Stroll Sock Yarn, 50g (211m/231yds), 75% superwash merino wool, 25% nylon, in the following shades:

- 1 ball of Pink (Dogwood Heather), shade 25603 (MC)
- 4m/4yds of Black, shade 23701 (CC1)
- 5.5m/6yds of Deep Pink (Rouge), shade 25020 (CC2)

Needles

- 2.25mm (US 1) double-pointed needles (set of 4) or circular needle
- 2.75mm (US 2) double-pointed needles (set of 4) or circular needle
- 3.75mm (US 5) needle (only used for loose cast off)

Extras

- Stitch holder
- Stitch marker
- Wool/tapestry needle

Pattern Notes

For all techniques used in this pattern, refer to Techniques for full instructions.

Socks are worked from the toe up.

Instructions are given for using double-pointed needles. If using a circular needle for the magic loop method, note that the instructions have the heel split over Needles 1 and 2, and the instep on Needle 3.

PIG SOCKS (MAKE TWO ALIKE)

TOE

Use Judy's Magic Cast-on method (see Techniques).

With 2.75mm needles and Pink (MC), cast on 16(20:20:24:24) sts over 2 needles – 8(10:10:12:12)sts on each needle.

Rnd 1 Knit.

Next, divide the 8(10:10:12:12)sts on first needle evenly over 2 dpns for the bottom of sock/heel. These are now called Needle 1 and Needle 2. Leave the last 8(10:10:12:12)sts on third dpn for top of sock/instep. This is now called Needle 3.

Now start increase rounds as follows (see Techniques: Toe Increases).

Rnd 2 Starting with Needle 1: kfb, knit to last st on Needle 2, kfb in last st; on Needle 3: kfb, knit to last st on Needle 3, kfb in last st – 20(24:24:28:28)sts.

Rep *Rnds 1-2* until you have 44(48:52:56:60)sts in total.

FOOT

For a generic foot size, knit until foot measures approximately 12.75(15.25:17.75:19:21)cm (5(6:7:7½:8¼)in) from cast on, or for best fit, knit until foot measures 3.75(3.75:4.5:4.5:4.5)cm (1½(1½:1¾:1¾:1¾)in) less than your total foot length.

HEEL

Continue in Pink (MC).

Work in rows over Needles 1 & 2.

See Techniques: Wrap and Turn for W&T.

Bottom half of heel

Row 1 Starting with Needle 1: knit to last st on Needle 2, W&T.

Row 2 Purl to last st on Needle 1 (this is last st with wrong side facing), W&T.

Row 3 Knit to 1 st before the last wrapped st of the heel, W&T.

Row 4 Purl to 1 st before the last wrapped st of the heel, W&T.

Rep *Rows 3-4* until 6(8:8:8:10)sts remain unworked in the middle of the heel. Bottom half of heel is now complete.

Top half of heel

See Techniques: Wrap and Turn for picking up wrapped stitches.

Row 1 Knit to first wrapped st, pick up wrapped st and knit it together with st on needle, W&T the next st (this st now has 2 wraps).

Row 2 Purl to first wrapped st, pick up wrapped st and purl it together with st on needle, W&T the next st (this st now has 2 wraps).

Row 3 Knit to st with double wrap. Pick up both wraps and knit them together with st on needle, W&T the next st.

Row 4 Purl to st with double wrap. Pick up both wraps and purl them together with st on needle, W&T the next st.

Rep *Rows 3-4* until there is 1 double wrap left on each side of heel.

Next row Rep *Row 3*, wrapping 1 st from top of sock/instep.

Next row Rep *Row 4*, wrapping 1 st from top of sock/instep.

LEG

Rnd 1 Begin to knit sock in the round again. When you come to the wrapped sts on the instep, pick up these wraps and knit them together with their respective sts.

Continue to knit until sock measures 12.75(14:15.25:15.25:16.5) cm (5(5½:6:6:6½)in) from bottom of heel, or desired length, noting that ribbing will add 2cm (¾in).

Pig Face for all sizes

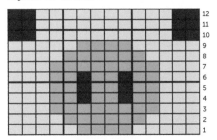

Pig Heel for all sizes

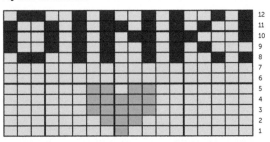

MC ☐   CC1 ■   CC2 ▨

CUFF

Change to 2.25mm needles and work in (k1, p1) rib for 2cm (¾in), working to last 1(2:2:2:2)sts on last round.

EARS

When casting off in rib (see Techniques: Casting Off in Rib), you will need to cast off very loosely to ensure your sock will fit your leg, therefore a much larger needle is recommended – try using a 3.75mm needle to cast off and create the perfect tension.

If you want to cast off loosely using your own preferred method, feel free to ignore the needle changing instructions referenced for casting off. If knitting for yourself you can try the sock on before knitting the ears to make sure you are happy with your casting off tension.

With 3.75mm needle, cast off the next 1(2:2:2:2)sts, then cast off all sts on Needles 1 & 2, and cast off 1(2:2:2:2)sts from Needle 3 – 20(20:22:24:26)sts remaining (including 1 st on right-hand needle).

Change back to 2.25mm needles and work in rib as established for 8 sts (9 sts are now on right-hand needle). Place these 9 sts just worked onto a stitch holder.

With 3.75mm needle, cast off 2(2:4:6:8)sts, change to 2.25mm needles and work in rib as established, for the last 8 sts - 9 sts remaining.

Left ear

Using a second 2.25mm needle, pick up 9 sts behind 9 sts just worked (see Techniques: Ears, picking up stitches for ears) – 18 sts.

Change to 2.75mm needles. Work in the round, starting at one side of ear, using a stitch marker to mark the start of the round.

Work left ear following instructions given for pointed ears (see Techniques: Ears).

Right ear

Transfer 9 sts from stitch holder to a 2.25mm needle. Using a second 2.25mm needle, pick up 9 sts behind 9 live sts (see Techniques: Ears, picking up stitches for ears) – 18 sts.

Change to 2.75mm needles. Work in the round, starting at one side of ear.

Work right ear following instructions given for pointed ears (see Techniques: Ears).

ADDING DETAILS

Using duplicate stitch (see Techniques: Duplicate Stitch), embroider colour charts onto socks as follows:

Face

Apply face chart on centre front of sock, to sit 2 rows below ribbing.

Heel

Apply heel chart on centre back heel, aligning top row of chart with first round of leg.

FINISHING

Weave all ends into wrong side and trim.

Block your socks (see Techniques: Blocking).

As a variation, you could leave out the heart stitching and add another row of 'OINK!' instead.

Hug Me
ANKLE SOCKS

Your feet will be so happy to be hugged by these adorable koala socks with their rosy, heart-shaped cheeks. These lovable critters will cuddle your feet as you walk, run and jump, and their sweet little rounded ears add a touch of cuteness.

SIZES

XS(S:M:L:XL) – see Size Chart for detailed measurements.
Sock Height: 14.5(15.75:17:17:18.5)cm (5¾(6¼:6¾:6¾:7¼)in).

DIFFICULTY LEVEL

TENSION

31 sts and 42 rows to measure 10 x 10cm (4 x 4in), over stocking stitch, using 2.75mm needles (or size needed to achieve correct tension).

Pattern Notes

For all techniques used in this pattern, refer to Techniques for full instructions.

Socks are worked from the toe up.

Instructions are given for using double-pointed needles. If using a circular needle for the magic loop method, note that the instructions have the heel split over Needles 1 and 2, and the instep on Needle 3.

You will need

Yarn

Knit Picks Stroll Sock Yarn, 50g (211m/231yds), 75% superwash merino wool, 25% nylon, in the following shades:

- 1 ball of Grey (Dove Heather), shade 25023 (MC)
- 46m/50yds of Pink (Dogwood Heather), shade 25603 (CC1)
- 7.5m/8yds of Black, shade 23701 (CC2)
- 4.5m/5yds of White, shade 26082 (CC3)

Needles

- 2.25mm (US 1) double-pointed needles (set of 4) or circular needle
- 2.75mm (US 2) double-pointed needles (set of 4) or circular needle
- 3.75mm (US 5) needle (only used for loose cast off)

Extras

- Stitch holder
- Stitch marker
- Wool/tapestry needle

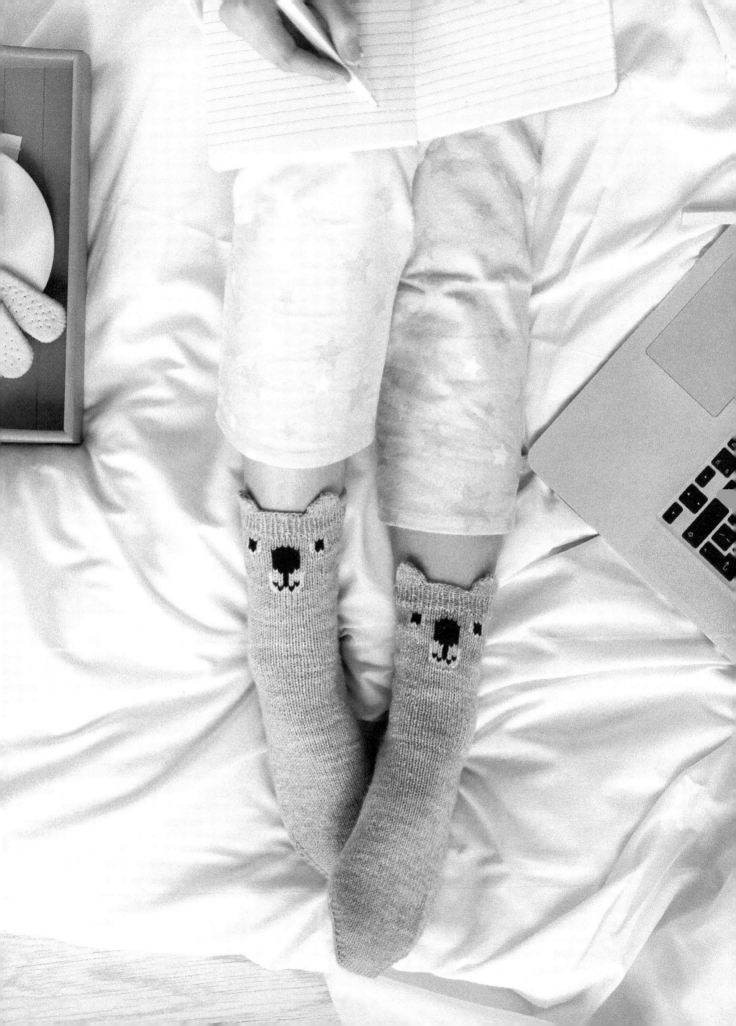

KOALA SOCKS (MAKE TWO ALIKE)

TOE

Use Judy's Magic Cast-on method (see Techniques).

With 2.75mm needles and Pink (CC1), cast on 16(20:20:24:24) sts over 2 needles – 8(10:10:12:12)sts on each needle.

Rnd 1 Knit.

Next, divide the 8(10:10:12:12)sts on first needle evenly over 2 dpns for the bottom of sock/heel. These are now called Needle 1 and Needle 2. Leave the last 8(10:10:12:12)sts on third dpn for top of sock/instep. This is now called Needle 3.

Now start increase rounds as follows (see Techniques: Toe Increases).

Rnd 2 Starting with Needle 1: kfb, knit to last st on Needle 2, kfb in last st; on Needle 3: kfb, knit to last st on Needle 3, kfb in last st – 20(24:24:28:28)sts.

Rep *Rnds 1-2* until you have 44(48:52:56:60)sts in total.

FOOT

Change to Grey (MC).

For a generic foot size, knit until foot measures approximately 12.75(15.25:17.75:19:21)cm (5(6:7:7½:8¼)in) from cast on, or for best fit, knit until foot measures 3.75(3.75:4.5:4.5:4.5)cm (1½(1½:1¾:1¾:1¾)in) less than your total foot length.

HEEL

Change to Pink (CC1).

Work in rows over Needles 1 & 2. See Techniques: Wrap and Turn for W&T.

Bottom half of heel

Row 1 Starting with Needle 1: knit to last st on Needle 2, W&T.

Row 2 Purl to last st on Needle 1 (this is last st with wrong side facing), W&T.

Row 3 Knit to 1 st before the last wrapped st of the heel, W&T.

Row 4 Purl to 1 st before the last wrapped st of the heel, W&T.

Rep *Rows 3-4* until 6(8:8:8:10)sts remain unworked in the middle of the heel. Bottom half of heel is now complete.

Top half of heel

See Techniques: Wrap and Turn for picking up wrapped stitches.

Row 1 Knit to first wrapped st, pick up wrapped st and knit it together with st on needle, W&T the next st (this st now has 2 wraps).

Row 2 Purl to first wrapped st, pick up wrapped st and purl it together with st on needle, W&T the next st (this st now has 2 wraps).

Row 3 Knit to st with double wrap. Pick up both wraps and knit them together with st on needle, W&T the next st.

Row 4 Purl to st with double wrap. Pick up both wraps and purl them together with st on needle, W&T the next st.

Rep *Rows 3-4* until there is 1 double wrap left on each side of heel.

Change back to Grey for next row (note that the first stitch will be skipped when working this row; that's ok!).

Next row Rep *Row 3*, wrapping 1 st from top of sock/instep.

Next row Rep *Row 4*, wrapping 1 st from top of sock/instep.

LEG

Rnd 1 Begin to knit sock in the round again. When you come to the wrapped sts on the instep, pick up these wraps and knit them together with their respective sts.

Continue to knit until sock measures 12.75(14:15.25:15.25:16.5)cm (5(5½:6:6:6½)in) from bottom of heel, or desired length, noting that ribbing will add 2cm (¾in).

Koala Face for sizes M-XL

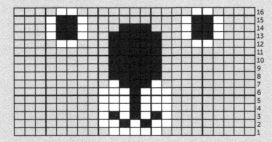

Koala Face for sizes XS-S

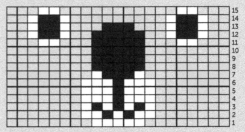

MC ☐   CC2 ■   CC1 ☐   CC3 ☐

Koala Heel for all sizes

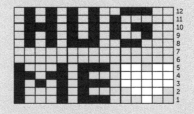

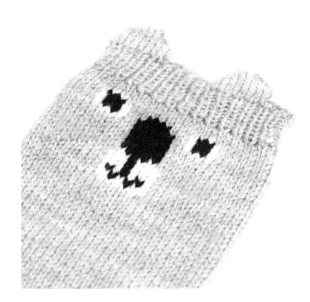

CUFF

Change to 2.25mm needles and work in (k1, p1) rib for 2cm (¾in), working to last 1(2:2:2:2)sts on last round.

EARS

When casting off in rib (see Techniques: Casting Off in Rib), you will need to cast off very loosely to ensure your sock will fit your leg, therefore a much larger needle is recommended – try using a 3.75mm needle to cast off and create the perfect tension.

If you want to cast off loosely using your own preferred method, feel free to ignore the needle changing instructions referenced for casting off. If knitting for yourself you can try the sock on before knitting the ears to make sure you are happy with your casting off tension.

With 3.75mm needle, cast off the next 1(2:2:2:2)sts, then cast off all sts on Needles 1 & 2, and cast off 1(2:2:2:2)sts from Needle 3 – 20(20:22:24:26)sts remaining (including 1 st on right-hand needle).

Change back to 2.25mm needles and work in rib as established for 8 sts (9 sts are now on right-hand needle). Place these 9 sts just worked onto a stitch holder.

With 3.75mm needle, cast off 2(2:4:6:8)sts, change to 2.25mm needles and work in rib as established, for the last 8 sts - 9 sts remaining.

Left ear

Using a second 2.25mm needle, pick up 9 sts behind 9 sts just worked (see Techniques: Ears, picking up stitches for ears) – 18 sts.

Change to 2.75mm needles. Work in the round, starting at one side of ear, using a stitch marker to mark the start of the round.

Work left ear following instructions given for rounded ears (see Techniques: Ears).

Right ear

Transfer 9 sts from stitch holder to a 2.25mm needle. Using a second 2.25mm needle, pick up 9 sts behind 9 live sts (see Techniques: Ears, picking up stitches for ears) – 18 sts.

Change to 2.75mm needles. Work in the round, starting at one side of ear.

Work right ear following instructions given for rounded ears (see Techniques: Ears).

ADDING DETAILS

Using duplicate stitch (see Techniques: Duplicate Stitch), embroider colour charts onto socks as follows:

Face

Choose face chart according to size knitted and apply on centre front of sock, to sit 2 rows below ribbing.

Heel

Apply heel chart on centre back heel, using contrast heel as a guide.

FINISHING

Weave all ends into wrong side and trim.

Block your socks (see Techniques: Blocking).

You can choose to omit the duplicate stitch text on the heel if you prefer.

Meow
LONG SOCKS

What better way to show your love and devotion to your feline friends than by wearing these quirky knee-high cat socks. Not only will your friends admire your amazing knitting talents, they will secretly be hoping that you'll knit them a pair too.

SIZES

S(M:L:XL) – see Size Chart for detailed measurements.
Sock Height: 30(35:40:42.5)cm (11¾(13¾:15¾:16¾)in).

DIFFICULTY LEVEL

TENSION

31 sts and 42 rows to measure 10 x 10cm (4 x 4in), over stocking stitch, using 2.75mm needles (or size needed to achieve correct tension).

You will need

Yarn

Knit Picks Stroll Sock Yarn, 50g (211m/231yds), 75% superwash merino wool, 25% nylon, in the following shades:

- 2 balls of Dark Grey (Basalt Heather), shade 24593 (MC)
- 7.5m/8yds of Pink (Dogwood Heather), shade 25603 (CC1)
- 5.5m/6yds of White, shade 26082 (CC2)

Needles

- 2.25mm (US 1) double-pointed needles (set of 4) or circular needle
- 2.75mm (US 2) double-pointed needles (set of 4) or circular needle
- 3.75mm (US 5) needle (only used for loose cast off)

Extras

- Stitch holder
- Stitch marker
- Wool/tapestry needle

Pattern Notes

For all techniques used in this pattern, refer to Techniques for full instructions.

Socks are worked from the toe up.

Instructions are given for using double-pointed needles. If using a circular needle for the magic loop method, note that the instructions have the heel split over Needles 1 and 2, and the instep on Needle 3.

CAT SOCKS (MAKE TWO ALIKE)

TOE

Use Judy's Magic Cast-on method (see Techniques).

With 2.75mm needles and Dark Grey (MC), cast on 20(20:24:24)sts over 2 needles – 10(10:12:12)sts on each needle.

Rnd 1 Knit.

Next, divide the 10(10:12:12)sts on first needle evenly over 2 dpns for the bottom of sock/heel. These are now called Needle 1 and Needle 2. Leave the last 10(10:12:12)sts on third dpn for top of sock/instep. This is now called Needle 3.

Now start increase rounds as follows (see Techniques: Toe Increases).

Rnd 2 Starting with Needle 1: kfb, knit to last st on Needle 2, kfb in last st; on Needle 3: kfb, knit to last st on Needle 3, kfb in last st – 24(24:28:28)sts.

Rep *Rnds 1-2* until you have 48(52:56:60)sts in total.

FOOT

For a generic foot size, knit until foot measures approximately 15.25(17.75:19:21)cm (6(7:7½:8¼)in) from cast on, or for best fit, knit until foot measures 3.75(4.5:4.5:4.5)cm (1½(1¾:1¾:1¾) in) less than your total foot length.

HEEL

Continue in Dark Grey (MC).

Work in rows over Needles 1 & 2.

See Techniques: Wrap and Turn for W&T.

Bottom half of heel

Row 1 Starting with Needle 1: knit to last st on Needle 2, W&T.

Row 2 Purl to last st on Needle 1 (this is last st with wrong side facing), W&T.

Row 3 Knit to 1 st before the last wrapped st of the heel, W&T.

Row 4 Purl to 1 st before the last wrapped st of the heel, W&T.

Rep *Rows 3-4* until 8(8:8:10)sts remain unworked in the middle of the heel. Bottom half of heel is now complete.

Top half of heel

See Techniques: Wrap and Turn for picking up wrapped stitches.

Row 1 Knit to first wrapped st, pick up wrapped st and knit it together with st on needle, W&T the next st (this st now has 2 wraps).

Row 2 Purl to first wrapped st, pick up wrapped st and purl it together with st on needle, W&T the next st (this st now has 2 wraps).

Row 3 Knit to st with double wrap. Pick up both wraps and knit them together with st on needle, W&T the next st.

Row 4 Purl to st with double wrap. Pick up both wraps and purl them together with st on needle, W&T the next st.

Rep *Rows 3-4* until there is 1 double wrap left on each side of heel.

Next row Rep *Row 3*, wrapping 1 st from top of sock/instep.

Next row Rep *Row 4*, wrapping 1 st from top of sock/instep.

LEG

Rnd 1 Begin to knit sock in the round again. When you come to the wrapped sts on the instep, pick up these wraps and knit them together with their respective sts.

Continue to knit, until sock measures 12.75(14:15.25:16.5)cm (5(5½:6:6½)in) from bottom of heel.

INCREASES

Increase Round Starting with Needle 1: kfb, knit to last st on Needle 2, kfb in last st; on Needle 3: kfb, knit to last st on Needle 3, kfb in last st – 52(56:60:64)sts.

Cat Face for all sizes

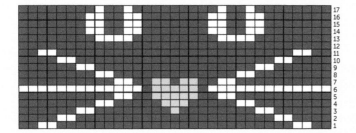

Cat Heel for all sizes

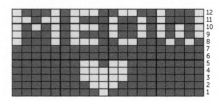

MC ■ CC1 ▨ CC2 □

Continue to knit in the round, repeating the Increase Round every 12th(14th:12th:12th) round, another 4(4:5:5) times – 68(72:80:84)sts.

Continue to knit in the round, until sock measures 28(33:38:40.5)cm (11(13:15:16in) from bottom of heel or desired length, noting that ribbing will add 2cm (¾in).

CUFF

Change to 2.25mm needles and work in (k1, p1) rib for 2cm (¾in), working to last 3(4:5:6)sts on last round.

EARS

When casting off in rib (see Techniques: Casting Off in Rib), you will need to cast off very loosely to ensure your sock will fit your leg, therefore a much larger needle is recommended – try using a 3.75mm needle to cast off and create the perfect tension.

If you want to cast off loosely using your own preferred method, feel free to ignore the needle changing instructions referenced for casting off. If knitting for yourself you can try the sock on before knitting the ears to make sure you are happy with your casting off tension.

With 3.75mm needle, cast off the next 3(4:5:6)sts, then cast off all sts on Needles 1 & 2, and cast off 3(4:5:6)sts from Needle 3 – 28(28:30:30)sts remaining (including 1 st on right-hand needle).

Change back to 2.25mm needles and work in rib as established for 8 sts (9 sts are now on right-hand needle). Place these 9 sts just worked onto a stitch holder.

With 3.75mm needle, cast off 10(10:12:12)sts, change to 2.25mm needles and work in rib as established, for the last 8 sts - 9 sts remaining.

Left ear

Using a second 2.25mm needle, pick up 9 sts behind 9 sts just worked (see Techniques: Ears, picking up stitches for ears) – 18 sts.

Change to 2.75mm needles. Work in the round, starting at one side of ear.

Work left ear following instructions given for pointed ears (see Techniques: Ears).

Right ear

Transfer 9 sts from stitch holder to a 2.25mm needle. Using a second 2.25mm needle, pick up 9 sts behind 9 live sts (see Techniques: Ears, picking up stitches for ears) – 18 sts.

Change to 2.75mm needles. Work in the round, starting at one side of ear, using a stitch marker to mark the start of the round.

Work right ear following instructions given for pointed ears (see Techniques: Ears).

ADDING DETAILS

Using duplicate stitch (see Techniques: Duplicate Stitch), embroider colour charts onto socks as follows:

Face

Apply face chart on centre front of sock, to sit 5 rows below ribbing.

Heel

Apply heel chart on centre back heel, aligning top row of chart with first round of leg.

FINISHING

Weave all ends into wrong side and trim.

Block your socks (see Techniques: Blocking).

~Hoot~
LONG SOCKS

Relax by the fire after a long day with these colourful sleepy owl socks. Have a hoot playing around with your favourite colour combinations and learn how to create a jogless stripe for the perfect finish. Team these with a pair of cat socks to create a The Owl and The Pussycat duo.

SIZES

S(M:L:XL) – see Size Chart for detailed measurements.
Sock Height: 30(35:40:42.5)cm (11¾(13¾:15¾:16¾)in).

DIFFICULTY LEVEL

TENSION

31 sts and 42 rows to measure 10 x 10cm (4 x 4in), over stocking stitch, using 2.75mm needles (or size needed to achieve correct tension).

Pattern Notes

For all techniques used in this pattern. refer to Techniques for full instructions.

Socks are worked from the toe up.

Instructions are given for using double-pointed needles. If using a circular needle for the magic loop method. note that the instructions have the heel split over Needles 1 and 2. and the instep on Needle 3.

You will need

Yarn

Knit Picks Stroll Sock Yarn, 50g (211m/231yds), 75% superwash merino wool, 25% nylon, in the following shades:

- 2 balls of Purple (Duchess Heather), shade 24594 (MC)
- 1 ball of Deep Pink (Rouge) shade 25020 (CC1)
- 9m/10yds of White, shade 26082 (CC2)
- 3.5m/4yds of Yellow (Dandelion), shade 25024 (CC3)
- 1.75m/2yds of Black, shade 23701 (CC4)

Needles

- 2.25mm (US 1) double-pointed needles (set of 4) or circular needle
- 2.75mm (US 2) double-pointed needles (set of 4) or circular needle
- 3.75mm (US 5) needle (only used for loose cast off)

Extras

- Stitch holder
- Stitch marker
- Wool/tapestry needle

OWL SOCKS (MAKE TWO ALIKE)

TOE

Use Judy's Magic Cast-on method (see Techniques).

With 2.75mm needles and Purple (MC), cast on 20(20:24:24) sts over 2 needles – 10(10:12:12)sts on each needle.

Rnd 1 Knit.

Next, divide the 10(10:12:12)sts on first needle evenly over 2 dpns for the bottom of sock/heel. These are now called Needle 1 and Needle 2. Leave the last 10(10:12:12)sts on third dpn for top of sock/instep. This is now called Needle 3.

Now start increase rounds as follows (see Techniques: Toe Increases).

Rnd 2 Starting with Needle 1: kfb, knit to last st on Needle 2, kfb in last st; on Needle 3: kfb, knit to last st on Needle 3, kfb in last st – 24(24:28:28)sts.

Rep *Rnds 1-2* until you have 48(52:56:60)sts in total.

FOOT

Change to Deep Pink (CC1) and continue to knit in the round, working in stripe pattern of 4 rows Deep Pink (CC1)/4 rows Purple (MC) throughout using the jogless stripe method (see Techniques: Jogless Stripes) and carrying the yarn not in use along the inside of your sock.

For a generic foot size, knit until foot measures approximately 15.25(17.75:19:21)cm (6(7:7½:8¼)in) from cast on, or for best fit, knit until foot measures 3.75(4.5:4.5:4.5)cm (1½(1¾:1¾:1¾)in) less than your total foot length. End after working only 2 rounds of Purple (MC) stripe pattern, and work heel in Purple (MC).

HEEL

Continue in Purple (MC).

Work in rows over Needles 1 & 2. See Techniques: Wrap and Turn for W&T.

Bottom half of heel

Row 1 Starting with Needle 1: knit to last st on Needle 2, W&T.

Row 2 Purl to last st on Needle 1 (this is last st with wrong side facing), W&T.

Row 3 Knit to 1 st before the last wrapped st of the heel, W&T.

Row 4 Purl to 1 st before the last wrapped st of the heel, W&T.

Rep *Rows 3-4* until 8(8:8:10)sts remain unworked in the middle of the heel. Bottom half of heel is now complete.

Top half of heel

See Techniques: Wrap and Turn for picking up wrapped stitches.

Row 1 Knit to first wrapped st, pick up wrapped st and knit it together with st on needle, W&T the next st (this st now has 2 wraps).

Row 2 Purl to first wrapped st, pick up wrapped st and purl it together with st on needle, W&T the next st (this st now has 2 wraps).

Row 3 Knit to st with double wrap. Pick up both wraps and knit them together with st on needle, W&T the next st.

Row 4 Purl to st with double wrap. Pick up both wraps and purl them together with st on needle, W&T the next st.

Rep *Rows 3-4* until there is 1 double wrap left on each side of heel.

Next row Rep *Row 3*, wrapping 1 st from top of sock/instep.

Next row Rep *Row 4*, wrapping 1 st from top of sock/instep.

LEG

Rnd 1 Continue in Purple (MC) and knit 1 round and when you come to the wrapped sts on the instep, pick up these wraps and knit them together with their respective sts.

Work 1 more round in Purple (MC) then continue in stripe pattern as established until sock measures 12.75(14:15.25:16.5) cm (5(5½:6:6½)in) from bottom of heel ending after 2nd round of any stripe colour, so that the 3rd round of the stripe is the increase round.

Owl Face for all sizes

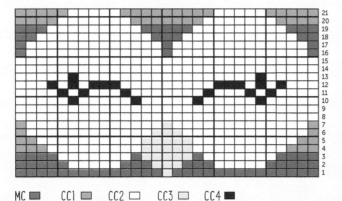

Owl Heel for all sizes

MC ■ CC1 ■ CC2 □ CC3 □ CC4 ■

INCREASES

Increase Round Starting with Needle 1: kfb, knit to last st on Needle 2, kfb in last st; on Needle 3: kfb, knit to last st on Needle 3, kfb in last st – 52(56:60:64)sts.

Continue to knit in the round in stripe pattern, repeating the Increase Round every 12th(14th:12th:12th) round, another 4(4:5:5) times – 68(72:80:84)sts.

Continue to knit in the round in stripe pattern, until sock measures 28(33:38:40.5)cm 11(13:15:16in) from bottom of heel or desired length, noting that ribbing will add 2cm (¾in). End after working a Deep Pink (CC1) stripe.

CUFF

Change to Purple (MC) and 2.25mm needles. Knit 1 round.

Work in (k1, p1) rib for 2cm (¾in), working to last 3(4:5:6)sts on last round.

EARS

When casting off in rib (see Techniques: Casting Off in Rib), you will need to cast off very loosely to ensure your sock will fit your leg, therefore a much larger needle is recommended – try using a 3.75mm needle to cast off and create the perfect tension.

If you want to cast off loosely using your own preferred method, feel free to ignore the needle changing instructions referenced for casting off. If knitting for yourself you can try the sock on before knitting the ears to make sure you are happy with your casting off tension.

With 3.75mm needle, cast off the next 3(4:5:6)sts, then cast off all sts on Needles 1 & 2, and cast off 3(4:5:6)sts from Needle 3 – 28(28:30:30)sts remaining (including 1 st on right-hand needle).

Change back to 2.25mm needles and work in rib as established for 8 sts (9 sts are now on right-hand needle). Place these 9 sts just worked onto a stitch holder.

With 3.75mm needle, cast off 10(10:12:12)sts, change to 2.25mm needles and work in rib as established, for the last 8 sts - 9 sts remaining.

Left ear

Using a second 2.25mm needle, pick up 9 sts behind 9 sts just worked (see Techniques: Ears, picking up stitches for ears) – 18 sts.

Change to 2.75mm needles. Work in the round, starting at one side of ear.

Work left ear following instructions given for pointed ears (see Techniques: Ears).

Right ear

Transfer 9 sts from stitch holder to a 2.25mm needle. Using a second 2.25mm needle, pick up 9 sts behind 9 live sts (see Techniques: Ears, picking up stitches for ears) – 18 sts.

Change to 2.75mm needles. Work in the round, starting at one side of ear.

Work right ear following instructions given for pointed ears (see Techniques: Ears).

ADDING DETAILS

Using duplicate stitch (see Techniques: Duplicate Stitch), embroider colour charts onto socks as follows:

Face

Apply face chart on centre front of sock, to sit 2 rows below ribbing.

Note that the stripes on the chart in purple and pink are for background reference only and do not need to be stitched.

Heel

Apply heel chart on centre back heel, placing chart 2 rows below the first Deep Pink (CC1) stripe of the leg.

FINISHING

Weave all ends into wrong side and trim.

Block your socks (see Techniques: Blocking).

Rawr LONG SOCKS

Take your socks to a whole new level of snugness with these charming panda socks. Packed full of fun, they would make a great birthday gift for a special friend or family member and even though pandas are solitary creatures, this pair will be your friend for life.

SIZES

S(M:L:XL) – see Size Chart for generic measurements.
Sock Height: 30(35:40:42.5)cm (11¾(13¾:15¾:16¾)in).

DIFFICULTY LEVEL

TENSION

31 sts and 42 rows to measure 10 x 10cm (4 x 4in), over stocking stitch, using 2.75mm needles (or size needed to achieve correct tension).

Pattern Notes

For all techniques used in this pattern, refer to Techniques for full instructions.

Socks are worked from the toe up.

Instructions are given for using double-pointed needles. If using a circular needle for the magic loop method, note that the instructions have the heel split over Needles 1 and 2, and the instep on Needle 3.

You will need

Yarn

Knit Picks Stroll Sock Yarn, 50g (211m/231yds), 75% superwash merino wool, 25% nylon, in the following shades:

- 2 balls of White, shade 26082 (MC)
- 46m/50yds of Black, shade 23701 (CC1)
- 3.5m/4yds of Pink (Dogwood Heather), shade 25603 (CC2)

Needles

- 2.25mm (US 1) double-pointed needles (set of 4) or circular needle
- 2.75mm (US 2) double-pointed needles (set of 4) or circular needle
- 3.75mm (US 5) needle (only used for loose cast off)

Extras

- Stitch holder
- Stitch marker
- Wool/tapestry needle

RAWR SOCKS (MAKE TWO ALIKE)

TOE

Use Judy's Magic Cast-on method (see Techniques).

With 2.75mm needles and Black (CC1), cast on 20(20:24:24) sts over 2 needles – 10(10:12:12)sts on each needle.

Rnd 1 Knit.

Next, divide the 10(10:12:12)sts on first needle evenly over 2 dpns for the bottom of sock/heel. These are now called Needle 1 and Needle 2. Leave the last 10(10:12:12)sts on third dpn for top of sock/instep. This is now called Needle 3.

Now start increase rounds as follows (see Techniques: Toe Increases).

Rnd 2 Starting with Needle 1: kfb, knit to last st on Needle 2, kfb in last st; on Needle 3: kfb, knit to last st on Needle 3, kfb in last st – 24(24:28:28)sts.

Rep *Rnds 1-2* until you have 48(52:56:60)sts in total.

FOOT

Change to White (MC).

For a generic foot size, knit until foot measures approximately 15.25(17.75:19:21)cm (6(7:7½:8¼)in) from cast on, or for best fit, knit until foot measures 3.75(4.5:4.5:4.5)cm (1½(1¾:1¾:1¾)in) less than your total foot length.

HEEL

Continue in White (MC).

Work in rows over Needles 1 & 2.

See Techniques: Wrap and Turn for W&T.

Bottom half of heel

Row 1 Starting with Needle 1: knit to last st on Needle 2, W&T.

Row 2 Purl to last st on Needle 1 (this is last st with wrong side facing), W&T.

Row 3 Knit to 1 st before the last wrapped st of the heel, W&T.

Row 4 Purl to 1 st before the last wrapped st of the heel, W&T.

Rep *Rows 3-4* until 8(8:8:10)sts remain unworked in the middle of the heel. Bottom half of heel is now complete.

Top half of heel

See Techniques: Wrap and Turn for picking up wrapped stitches.

Row 1 Knit to first wrapped st, pick up wrapped st and knit it together with st on needle, W&T the next st (this st now has 2 wraps).

Row 2 Purl to first wrapped st, pick up wrapped st and purl it together with st on needle, W&T the next st (this st now has 2 wraps).

Row 3 Knit to st with double wrap. Pick up both wraps and knit them together with st on needle, W&T the next st.

Row 4 Purl to st with double wrap. Pick up both wraps and purl them together with st on needle, W&T the next st.

Rep *Rows 3-4* until there is 1 double wrap left on each side of heel.

Next row Rep *Row 3*, wrapping 1 st from top of sock/instep.

Next row Rep *Row 4*, wrapping 1 st from top of sock/instep.

Panda Face for all sizes

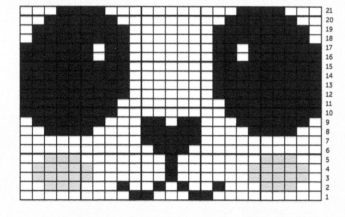

Panda Heel

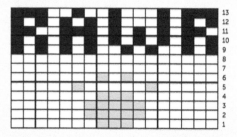

MC ☐   CC1 ■   CC2 ▨

LEG

Rnd 1 Begin to knit sock in the round again. When you come to the wrapped sts on the instep, pick up these wraps and knit them together with their respective sts (see Techniques: Wrap and Turn).

Continue to knit, until sock measures 12.75(14:15.25:16.5)cm (5(5½:6:6½)in) from bottom of heel.

INCREASES

Increase Round Starting with Needle 1: kfb, knit to last st on Needle 2, kfb in last st; on Needle 3: kfb, knit to last st on Needle 3, kfb in last st = 52(56:60:64)sts.

Continue to knit in the round, repeating the Increase Round every 12th(14th:12th:12th) round, another 4(4:5:5) times – 68(72:80:84)sts.

Continue to knit in the round, until sock measures 28(33:38:40.5)cm (11(13:15:16in) from bottom of heel or desired length, noting that ribbing will add 2cm (¾in).

CUFF

Change to 2.25mm needles and work in (k1, p1) rib for 2cm (¾in), working to last 3(4:5:6)sts on last round.

Cast off very loosely, using 3.75mm needles.

For a slightly stretchier cast-off, you can cast off in (k1, p1) rib (see Techniques: Casting Off in Rib) as well as using 3.75mm needles.

EARS

Mark 9 sts for each ear, centred on front of sock, evenly spaced, 10(10,12,12)sts apart.

Left ear

With 2.75mm needles and Black (CC1), and with front of sock facing, pick up 2 sts for every cast-off st by picking up and knitting 1 st from each leg of each cast-off st (see Techniques: Ears, picking up stitches for panda ears).

Work in the round, starting at one side of ear.

Work left ear following instructions given for rounded ears (see Techniques: Ears).

Repeat for right ear.

ADDING DETAILS

Using duplicate stitch (see Techniques: Duplicate Stitch), embroider colour charts onto socks as follows:

Face

Apply face chart on centre front of sock, to sit 2 rows below ribbing.

Heel

Apply heel chart on centre back heel, aligning top row of chart with first round of leg.

FINISHING

Weave all ends into wrong side and trim.

Block your socks (see Techniques: Blocking).

Techniques

JUDY'S MAGIC CAST-ON

This method of casting on was developed by Judy Becker (see Bibliography) and creates the first row of knitting, which is why it's completely invisible. It's the perfect method for toe-up sock knitting and is recommended for all the socks in this book. Follow the detailed steps below to cast on.

Step 1 Make a slip knot onto one dpn, leaving a long tail end of yarn **(A)**. This counts as the first stitch.

Step 2 Hold 2 dpns together, one above the other, with the needle holding the slip knot at the top. This is called Needle 2 and the other dpn is called Needle 1.

Step 3 In your free hand, hold the yarn, making sure that the tail end goes over your index finger and the working yarn (the yarn attached to the ball) goes over your thumb.

Step 4a Bring the tip of Needle 1 up and over the strand of yarn on your index finger.

Step 4b Feed the yarn over Needle 1 and in between the 2 needles, making a loop around Needle 1 **(B)**.

Step 4c Pull the loop snug, but not tight, around the needle.

You have cast one stitch on to Needle 1 (the stitch on Needle 2 is the slip knot).

Step 5 Bring Needle 2 downwards and in front of the tail on your thumb, then back up and under the yarn, feeding the yarn between the needles, making a loop around Needle 2. Pull the loop snug around the needle.

You have cast one stitch on to Needle 2.

There are now two stitches on Needle 2; the stitch you've just cast on plus the beginning slip knot.

Note that the top yarn strand always wraps around Needle 1 (which is the bottom needle), and the bottom yarn strand always wraps around Needle 2 (which is the top needle). It should help to remember this by repeating the following: Take the top needle around bottom yarn; take the bottom needle around top yarn. You will work in a figure of eight motion.

Step 6 Repeat Step 4 to cast a second stitch on to Needle 1 (take the bottom needle around top yarn).

Step 7 Repeat Step 5 to cast a third stitch on to Needle 2 (take the top needle around bottom yarn) **(C)**.

Step 8 Continue to repeat Steps 4 and 5, until you have cast on the desired number of stitches, ending with Step 4. You will now have the same number of stitches on each needle **(D)**. The side that is facing you is the right side of your knitting (the wrong side will feature a row of twists that look like purl bumps between the two needles).

Step 9 Start knitting: *Rnd 1*: Drop the yarn tail and let it dangle. Rotate the needles so that Needle 1 is now on the top. Pick up the working yarn and be sure that the yarn tail lies between the working yarn and the needle **(E)**.

Using a third dpn, knit the row of stitches from Needle 1. The first stitch will probably become loose while you are knitting it. Pull gently on the tail to tighten it back up **(F)**.

You will see a row of stitches appear between the two needles **(G)**.

Step 10 Rotate so that the working yarn is on the right and Needle 2 is on the top. Use spare dpn to knit the stitches from Needle 2.

You have completed one round and are back where you started.

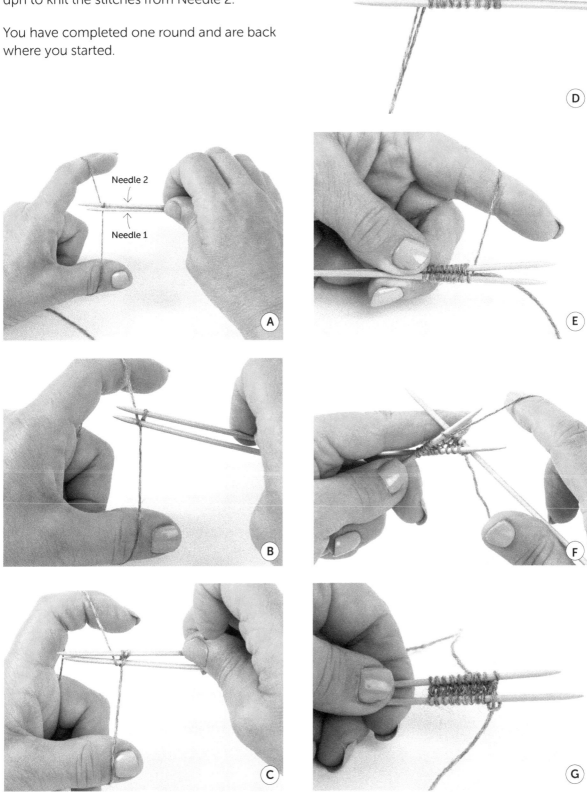

TOE INCREASES

Once you have cast on and knitted 1 round, you are ready to start increasing for the toe. But before the increases are worked, divide the stitches on your first needle over 2 dpns for the bottom of the sock/heel. These are now called Needle 1 and Needle 2. Leave all of the stitches as they are on the remaining dpn for the top of sock/instep.

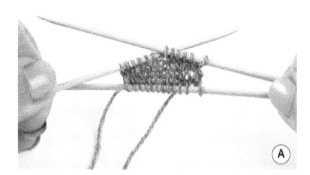

For increasing, a simple increase of kfb is used. Kfb is the abbreviation for 'knit into the front and back of the stitch' (see Increasing – kfb). This increases your stitch count by 1 stitch.

After working the toe increases as specified in the pattern, your toe section will start to look like this:

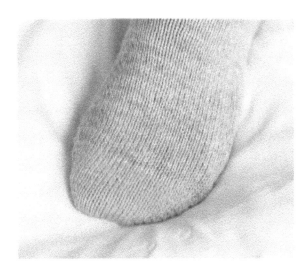

You can use a different colour for the toe to add more detail to your socks.

EARS

PICKING UP STITCHES FOR EARS

Each pair of cute critters has their own matching ears. Except for the panda, these ears are worked in the round from two sets of 9 sts that remain after the cuff cast off, as follows:

Step 1 After casting off for the cuff you will have a set of 9 sts on a stitch holder and 9 sts left on a 2.25mm (US 1) dpn.

Using a second 2.25mm needle, pick up 9 sts behind the last set of 9 sts that remain on dpn, after the cuff cast off, as follows:

Turn sock so that the wrong side of sock is facing (so you can see the inside of the sock). Pick up each purl ridge that sits below the live purl stitches of the rib and pick up the left leg of the 'V' of the knit stitch that sits below the live knit stitches of the rib **(A and B)**.

Step 2 You will now have 18 sts, ready to knit in the round for the ear **(C)**.

Step 3 Knit your ear according to the instructions that follow, for either a pointed ear or a rounded ear (as specified within the pattern being used).

PICKING UP STITCHES FOR PANDA EARS

Step 1 Place needle through front leg of cast-off stitch **(A)**. Wrap Black yarn around needle **(B)** and pull through. You have picked up 1 st **(C)**.

Step 2 Place needle through back leg of cast-off st **(D)**. Wrap yarn around needle and pull through. You have now picked up 2 sts from 1 cast-off stitch **(E)**.

Step 3 Repeat Steps 1 to 4 for each of the next 8 sts to create 18 sts in total from 9 cast-off stitches **(F)**.

Step 4 Turn work so back of sock is facing. Transfer sts to 2 larger needles, placing 1st st on back needle, then 2nd st on front needle **(G)**, alternating every st until all sts are transferred – 9 sts on each needle **(H)**.

Now work as given for rounded ears (see To Knit Rounded Ears).

E

F

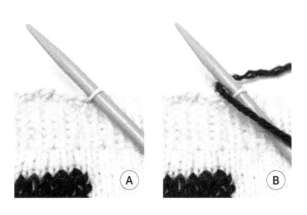

A

B

C

D

G

H

TO KNIT POINTED EARS (FOR FOX, PIG, CAT AND OWL) – MAKE TWO ALIKE

Rnds 1-2 Knit.

Rnd 3 [Ssk, k5, k2tog] twice – 14 sts.

Rnd 4 Knit.

Rnd 5 [Ssk, k3, k2tog] twice – 10 sts.

Rnd 6 Knit.

Rnd 7 [Ssk, k1, k2tog] twice – 6 sts.

Rnd 8 [Sl 1, k2tog, psso] twice – 2 sts.

Break off yarn, thread onto wool/tapestry needle and thread through remaining sts. Pull to gather and tie off. Weave tail end through to inside of ear, and weave in to wrong side of ribbing.

TO KNIT ROUNDED EARS (FOR KOALA AND PANDA) – MAKE TWO ALIKE

Rnds 1-4 Knit.

Rnd 5 [Ssk, k5, k2tog] twice – 14 sts.

Rnd 6 [Ssk, k3, k2tog] twice – 10 sts.

Rnd 7 [Ssk, k1, k2tog] twice – 6 sts.

Break off yarn, thread onto wool/tapestry needle and graft stitches together using Kitchener stitch (see Techniques: Kitchener Stitch). Weave tail end through to inside of ear, and weave in to wrong side of ribbing.

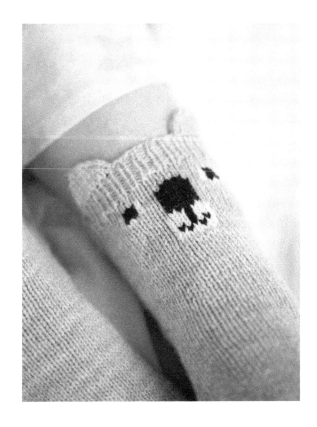

WRAP AND TURN

The wrap and turn method for the heels in this book allows you to add extra length or width to a small area of your knitting, but not to all of the project. The wrap and turn method is a form of short row knitting.

ON A KNIT ROW

Step 1 With yarn at the back of work, slip the next stitch from the left needle to the right needle purlwise.

Step 2 Bring the yarn forward, between the needles (as if you were going to purl).

Step 3 Slip the stitch from the right needle back to the left needle.

Step 4 Take the yarn between the needles to the back of work (as if you were going to knit).

Step 5 Turn your work so that the purl side is facing you, ready to purl the next row according to pattern.

ON A PURL ROW

Step 1 With yarn at the front, slip the next stitch purlwise from the left needle to the right needle.

Step 2 Take the yarn between the needles to the back (as if you were going to knit).

Step 3 Slip the stitch from the right needle back to the left needle.

Step 4 Bring the yarn to the front of the work (as if you were going to purl).

Step 5 Turn work so that the knit side is facing you, ready to knit the next row (according to pattern).

PICKING UP WRAPS ON THE KNIT SIDE

Step 1 When you reach the wrapped stitch, insert the right needle into the wrap, from front to back.

Step 2 Insert the right needle into the stitch that is wrapped. Then knit the wrap and the stitch together.

PICKING UP WRAPS ON THE PURL SIDE

Step 1 When you reach the wrapped stitch, insert the right needle into the wrap, from back to front.

Step 2 Place the wrap onto the left needle so that it sits over the top and behind the stitch that was wrapped. Then purl the wrap and the stitch together.

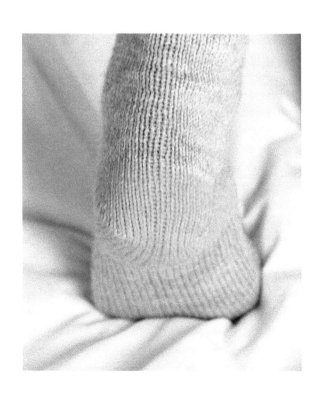

JOGLESS STRIPES

This method is used to help you create stripes that don't have a visible joining line where the colour is changed at the beginning of each round.

On the second round of every colour change, slip the first stitch purlwise (as if to purl), then knit as normal. It works like a charm!

CARRYING YARN

When working in stripes, you will need to carry your unused yarn along the wrong side of your work so that it is ready for use when needed.

To do this, when knitting with one stripe colour, you will need to wrap the other stripe colour behind your work as follows:

At the start of each round, wrap your working yarn clockwise around your non-working yarn before knitting the next round. When switching colours, place the previously used stripe colour over the new colour before knitting with the new colour.

BLOCKING

Once you've knitted up your socks, for best results, it is essential to block them out. This will help to smooth out your tension and give an even finish to your duplicate stitch patterns.

Step 1 Fill a small bowl with room temperature water and a squeeze of wool wash.

Step 2 Add your socks to the water and let them sit for 15-20 minutes. Do not agitate them or squeeze them with your hands because this may cause them to felt and shrink. Instead, gently move them around to make sure that the water soaks through.

Step 3 Very gently, squeeze out as much water as you can with your hands (do not wring or agitate) and lay your socks onto a clean towel.

Step 4 Begin to carefully roll up your socks in the towel.

Step 5 Press on the rolled up towel gently to squeeze out any excess water and then remove your socks and place them onto a sock blocker to dry.

KNIT STITCH

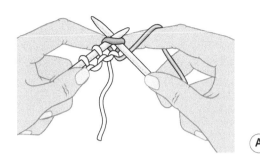

(A)

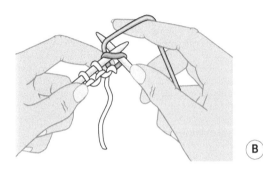

(B)

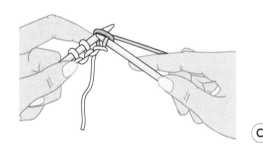

(C)

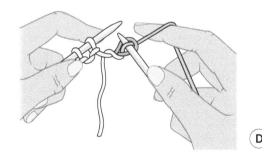

(D)

PURL STITCH

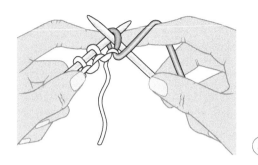

(A)

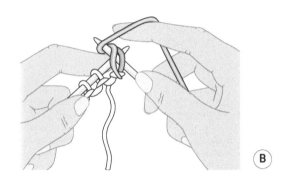

(B)

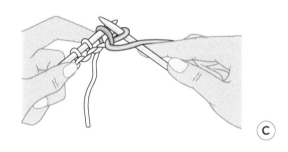

(C)

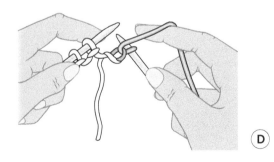

(D)

KNITTING IN THE ROUND

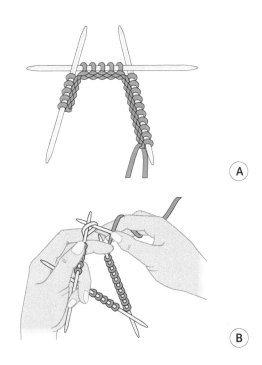

(A)

(B)

INCREASING - KFB

Knit into the front and back of next st, to increase 1 st.

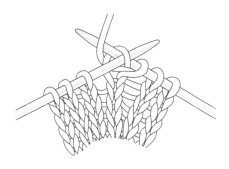

DECREASING - K2TOG

Knit 2 stitches together, to decrease 1 st.

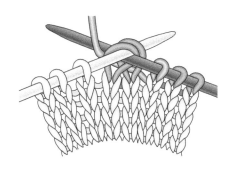

DECREASING - SSK

Slip, slip, knit 2 together through back loops, to decrease 1 st.

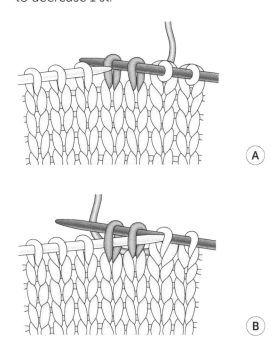

(A)

(B)

RIB STITCH - (K1, P1)

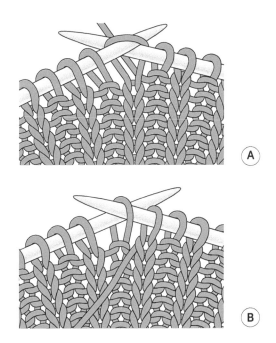

(A)

(B)

CASTING OFF IN RIB

For all socks, a (k1, p1) rib can also be used for the cuff, to create an extra-stretchy cast-off. You will need to cast off the cuff in rib stitch so that the cuff maintains enough elasticity to stretch over your calves and leg. To cast off in rib, work as follows:

Step 1 Knit first stitch.

Step 2 Purl next stitch. 2 stitches are now on right-hand needle and yarn is at the front.

Step 3 Use left-hand needle to lift the first (knit) stitch up and over the second (purl) stitch to cast it off.

Step 4 Take yarn to the back, between needles.

Step 5 Knit the next stitch. 2 stitches are now on right-hand needle and yarn is at the back.

Step 6 Use left-hand needle to lift the first stitch up and over the second stitch to cast it off.

Step 7 Bring yarn to front between needles.

Repeat Steps 2 to 7 until all of the stitches have been cast off and 1 stitch remains on needle. The last stitch is a purl stitch so you will end after Step 4. Cut yarn leaving a long tail end. Remove last stitch from needle and lengthen the loop so that it doesn't unravel. Thread yarn tail onto a wool needle and thread needle underneath the top loops of the first stitch that was cast off (inserting needle from front to back). Pull yarn through gently then thread yarn through last remaining stitch.

The first and last stitches of the round are now neatly joined. Weave tail end of yarn into wrong side of rib; secure firmly and fasten off.

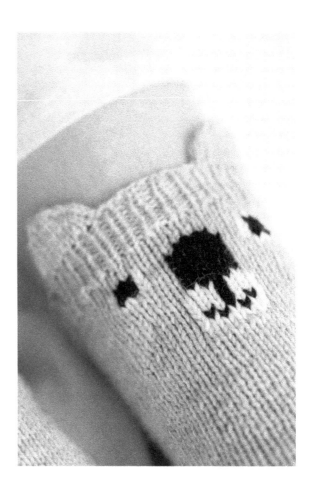

KITCHENER STITCH

Kitchener stitch (also called grafting) joins two sets of stitches that are still on needles (and haven't been cast off), by weaving yarn through the stitches, following the steps below. A knitted stitch is created between the two sets of stitches, which makes an invisible join.

Step 1 Hold the 2 sets of needles parallel, with wrong sides of knitting facing each other and right sides facing outwards, with the tips of the needles pointing in the same direction.

Step 2 Thread yarn from the back piece onto a wool/tapestry needle. Insert wool/tapestry needle into first stitch on front needle as if to purl. Pull yarn through, leaving the stitch on the needle **(A)**.

Step 3 Insert wool/tapestry needle into first stitch on back needle as if to knit. Pull yarn through, leaving the stitch on the needle **(B)**.

Step 4 Insert the wool/tapestry needle into the first stitch on the front needle as if to knit and slip it off the end of the needle **(C)**.

Step 5 Insert the wool/tapestry needle into the next stitch on the front needle as if to purl. Pull yarn through and this time leave the stitch on the needle **(D)**.

Step 6 Insert the wool/tapestry needle into the first stitch on the back needle as if to purl, and slip it off the end of the needle **(E)**.

Repeat Steps 3 to 6 until seam has been grafted together, stopping every couple of centimetres or inch to tighten up the stitches to create a tension that matches your knitting **(F)**.

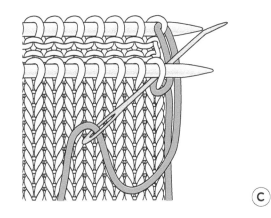

C

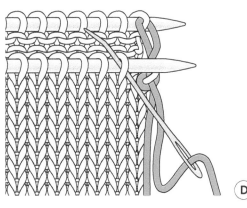

D

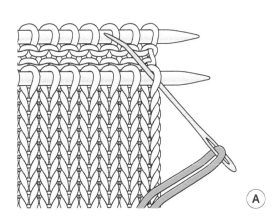

A

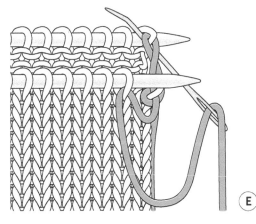

E

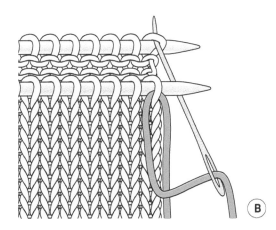

B

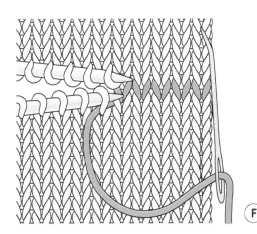

F

DUPLICATE STITCH

Duplicate stitch (also called Swiss darning) is a technique allowing you to add small areas of colour to the surface of your completed fabric. For best results, use yarn of a similar weight to your background fabric.

Step 1 Thread your needle with a long piece of contrast yarn and bring it through the 'V' below the first stitch to duplicate from the back to the front of your knitting **(A)**.

Step 2 Take the needle under both 'legs' of the stitch above the stitch to be duplicated, in the same direction as you will be working **(B)**.

Step 3 To finish, go back through the 'V' below the stitch to be duplicated, from front to back. Pull yarn gently, but not too tightly, so that it sits on top of the stitch being duplicated and covers as much of it as possible **(C)**.

Repeat across the row, following the chart you are duplicating, repeating steps for each stitch worked.

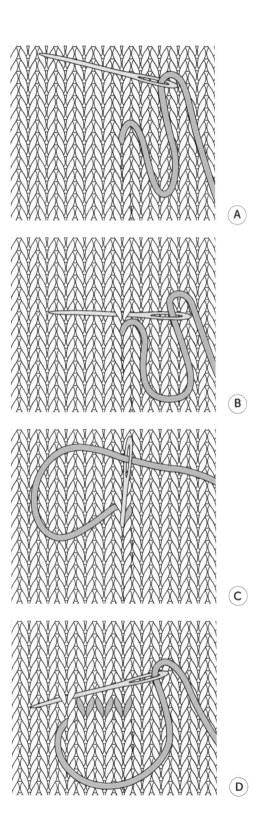

CHART TEMPLATES

Design your own animal faces using these blank templates! The coloured boxes are a guide to show you how wide the top of your sock is, which will help with plotting out your chart.

FACE CHART TEMPLATE (FOR KNEE-HIGH SOCKS)

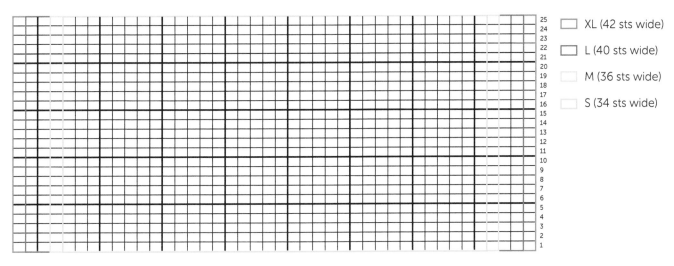

XL (42 sts wide)

L (40 sts wide)

M (36 sts wide)

S (34 sts wide)

FACE CHART TEMPLATE (FOR ANKLE SOCKS)

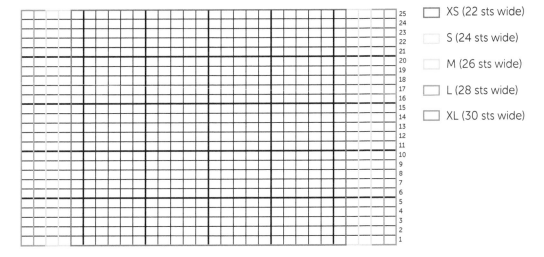

XS (22 sts wide)

S (24 sts wide)

M (26 sts wide)

L (28 sts wide)

XL (30 sts wide)

SUPPLIERS

Knit Picks - www.knitpicks.com

BIBLIOGRAPHY

Judy Becker, for Judy's Magic Cast-on, http://knitty.com/ISSUEspring06/FEATmagiccaston.html

ABOUT THE AUTHOR

Lauren has been knitting since she was 9, and working in New York City as a fashion designer for juniors and girls since 2005. She loves cats, purple and everything girly! Discover her patterns at girlyknits.com, read her blog at knittingisawesome.com, and find her on social media as @girlyknits.

ACKNOWLEDGMENTS

Thank you to everyone at F&W Media, from those who found my patterns to those who turned it into a book. I would like to thank my friends and family for supporting and encouraging me, and Knit Picks for their amazing partnership in all of my knitting endeavours. I would also like to thank my cat Ezzy for snuggling up with me while I knit, and inspiring my love for animals.

A SEWANDSO BOOK
© F&W Media International, Ltd 2018

SewandSo is an imprint of F&W Media International, Ltd
Pynes Hill Court, Pynes Hill, Exeter, EX2 5AZ, UK

F&W Media International, Ltd is a subsidiary of F+W Media, Inc
10151 Carver Road, Suite #200, Blue Ash, OH 45242, USA

Text and Designs © Lauren Riker 2018
Layout and Photography © F&W Media International, Ltd 2018

First published in the UK and USA in 2018

Lauren Riker has asserted her right to be identified as author of this work in accordance with the Copyright, Designs and Patents Act, 1988.

A catalogue record for this book is available from the British Library.

ISBN-13: 978-1-4463-0715-1 paperback
SRN: R8070 paperback

ISBN-13: 978-1-4463-7716-1 PDF
SRN: R8072 PDF

ISBN-13: 978-1-4463-7715-4 EPUB
SRN: R8071 EPUB

Content Director: Ame Verso
Acquisitions Editor: Sarah Callard
Managing Editor: Jeni Hennah
Project Editor: Lynne Rowe
Proofreader: Cheryl Brown
Design Manager: Lorraine Inglis
Designer: Sam Staddon
Photographer: Jason Jenkins
Production Manager: Beverley Richardson
Art Direction and Styling: Lorraine Inglis

F&W Media publishes high quality books on a wide range of subjects. For more great book ideas visit: www.sewandso.co.uk

Layout of the digital edition of this book may vary depending on reader hardware and display settings.

Lightning Source UK Ltd.
Milton Keynes UK
UKHW050447070219

336858UK00001B/24/P